The Poetic

Diary

Of

Love and Change

Clarissa O. Clemens

ISBN-13: 978-0615657493

ISBN-10: 0615657494

Hopeful Hearts Press

Table of Contents

Clarissa O. Clemens

DEDICATION

This book is for the healing of all the broken hearts
without hope. Writing these poems helped me to
find the strength and resolve that love was waiting
somewhere in the world for me to find, recapture,
and embrace.

I found love blossoming in myself first and then he
came along so that we could become one together
and apart.

Much to Do

Too personal to share

Too deep to dig out

Too far away to care

To sad to pout

Too much to do

To get anything done

To love to risk

To hurt to whisk

To stir up feelings

To heal after reeling

To take steps forward

To do it again

To look hope-ward

To try and sustain

To hold onto joy

To pave to ponder

To take off and fly

To let your heart wander

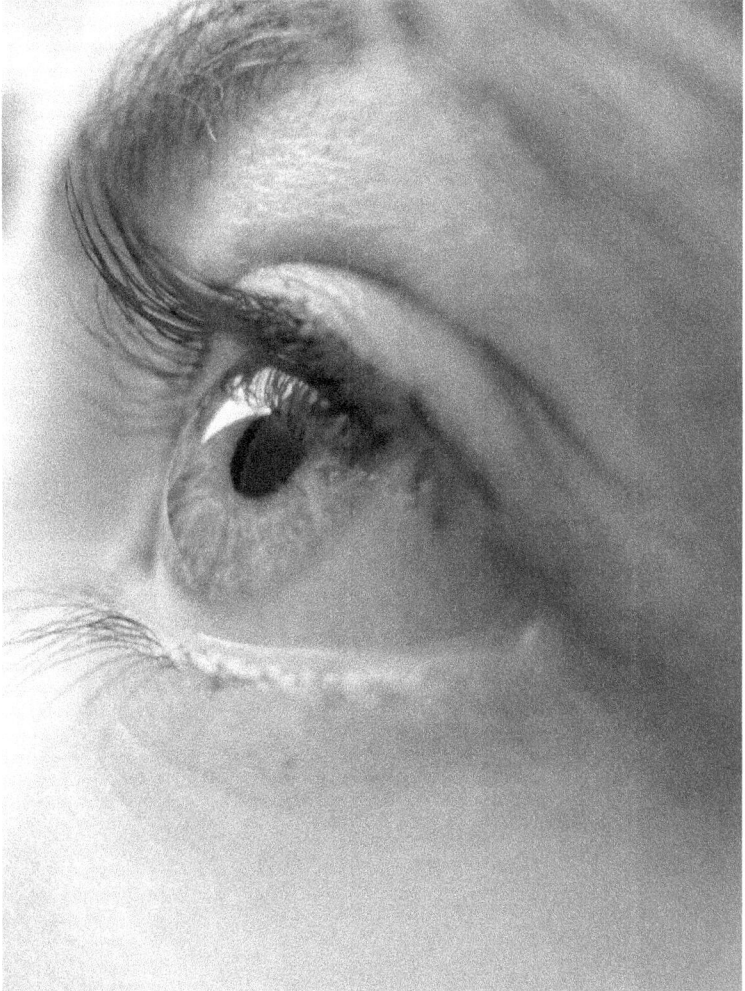

Abyss of Nothingness

Existing in the abyss of nothingness

Floating in the great beyond

Clinging to the feeling of weightlessness

Dreaming of the unbreakable bond

Sinking into swirling seas

Trusting the future to the powers that be

Twirling spirits creating clouds

Searching for you within the crowd

I find you peaceful waiting there

Our eyes connect in a loving stare

Warm embrace holds us tight

Not letting go, not losing sight

The fear of loss that weighed heavy on my heart

Has left me now to begin a new start

Swarming Humans

Swarming humans

Which one will you be?

Open heart in search of me

I'm here I'm joyful

Knowing you exist

Our paths true meeting

A fleeting glimpse

Feeling your touch

Is almost here

My core reaching out

Finding my sphere

Hold me feel my joy

For Life

For Love

For You

I am here

For Our Healing

So much anticipation

to see you for real

To look into your eyes

Now that you know

how I feel

I've opened my heart,

please enter gently

Pouring out our emotions,

Feeling you intently

You have entered inside

All fears pushed aside

You have nothing to lose

by giving yourself to me

Maybe the risk

and the vulnerability

But I know

God has given us this gift

This feeling

For our heart, for our health,

For our healing

It Will be Now, Then

Where are you?

My fingers reach out

Into voided space

How do I move on cue?

To coordinate

To be in a place

Where you might be

So I can glance your face

Expand the me

To become we

When will you get here?

Fate and Faith

Come into play

Almost sensing

You are in my range

But there you stay

Until the day

Living without you

Feels so strange

Confused in my brain

Feeling deranged

Do you really exist?

Do I try to persist?

Or allow it to unfold

Letting go

Release the hold

No direction

Can be made

The future

Is already unlade

Before me to follow

To fill out the hollow

Candle Lit Heart

When the weird disappeared

When the light came into sight

I saw your face

My heart began to race

I went towards you

Because I knew

Who you were

I felt the lure

Spirits already connected

Feeling affected

By the love you extend

My life starts to mend

Waiting for the right chance

To start our dance

Into your arms

Understanding those charms

Fully in sync

Nothing able to break the link

Keep the faith feel secure

The love between us is so pure

It has existed longer than we know

Opening up we let it flow

It flourishes it grows

and becomes a joyous being

Unto itself separate

When we open our eyes we are seeing

The candle has been lit

2 to 1

2 hearts 1 beat

2 lips will meet

2 birds 1 stone

2 never b alone

2 wills 1 goal

2 halves 1 whole

2 be in love

2 be as One

Precipice of Bliss

On the precipice of bliss

So anxious for your kiss

With all the words exchanged between us

Creating the bond of trust

Ready to rocket off into space

Holding a vivid image of your face

Firmly in my mind enshrined

The feeling of your being, so divine

Bubbling and brewing emotional stirring

Life, joy, and love occurring

Releasing and ready to fall

Headed toward giving you all

Of my heart, head, and hand

Softly into your soul I land

Sink to Think

As I think of you

My heart starts to sink

The tears fill my eyes

And I can't even think

All the years together

So happy and in sync

The walls went up

The distance grew

What happened to the

Man I knew

You're flying away

Paving a new path

Leaving us behind

Pulling at my hearts wrath

Slices of Visions

Slices of visions pop in my head

Seeing our moments spent in your bed

Vivid and warm feeling so real

Your sensuous touch my body to heal

Closing my eyes I see you right here

Off in my fantasy bringing you near

I whimper inside longing to find

Our lusting limbs intertwined

Your face before me in my mind

Falling into your eyes so blue so kind

Intense sparks of desire leaking a sigh

Lighting the fire feeling so high

Anticipation of our next meeting

My heart quickens in it's beating

Open and ready for you to arrive

Together our spirits are vibrant and alive

Wanting Weaving

Wanting to be loved so bad

Giving up the love I had

Weaving in and out of sad

Trying not to feel too mad

Tears so close and standing by

Through life I coast to flee to fly

Landing in a lover's heart I try

To settle in to stop the cry

But when I leave I'm still alone

The only connection becomes the phone

Ghostly voice softly moan

Tells me with the wind that's blown

Almost reaching almost home

The current future still unknown

What We Will Be

At the drop of a pin

The urges from within

Surge up my spine

Almost aligned

Overtaking my breath

Breathless I am left

Uttering your name

Emotions untamed

Grabbing your mind

With mine entwined

Submerged in the glow

Allowing the flow

Between you and me

We will just have to see

What we will be

Lips Longing Lustful

Are we ready for this?

So much anticipation

for your kiss

Nervous and excited

The idea of you sighted

But what about the real

With my imagination

you steal

Heart racing fast

Magnetism surpassed

Lips longing lustful

Giving in total and trustful

My eager pulse

does rush

Feeling my cheeks

as they blush

Warmth blankets my being

Sensuous and smooth

against you leaning

My face in your hands

Melted and waiting

for the kiss to land

The Life that I Need

Stress overwhelming

my life as a whole

Ripping and tearing

gaps in my soul

Security fleeting

flying away

Grabbing at its wings

begging it to stay

Trying to find my faith

as an anchor secure

My feet are searching

for a stationary floor

Old flower withering

Dying on the vine

New bloom so fresh

Opening divine

Picking and choosing

the life that I need

Will you love me and join me

when we are both freed?

Out of Whack

The drone of chatter

Numbs my brain

Climbing the ladder

Letting go of the pain

Train of life

Speeding toward a new track

Hurling me forward

Feeling out of whack

Grabbing at the rails

Mother earth at my feet

Releasing what ails

Turning my back on defeat

To be whole once more

Free and ready to open the door

Fragile Loving Heart

Forgive your futile frustrated expression

Heated under hot cinders of confliction

Shaped by your myriads of whirl-pooled thoughts

Baked inward from burnt exhaustion battles fought

Roasting a fragile loving heart with nervous

shrouds of doubt

Feelings of surety shrink under threat of drought

Relinquish volition surrender to pure unthinking

Allow joyous unyielding love unblinking

Gift of god given freely

Embraced inside feel the healing

Touch my life send us reeling

Absence of strife soaring sealing

Joy Love One

Tahoe Sparkle

Powdered sugar sprinkled pure

Above the crowds to find the cure

Sparkling diamond peaks of light

Reflected nature shimmery delight

Thoughts unwind, body relaxed

Gazing at the glistening tracks

Crisp cool breeze whispers by

Watching parasailors float in the sky

Closing my eyes, imagining you here

Holding your hand, holding you dear

Lapping waves caress my feet

Sunbeams cascade summers sweet

Melted cream drips down my hand

Toes wiggling in warm smooth sand

Pressures gone released from sight

Spirits soaring my heart takes flight

Back Burner

Put the stress on the back burner

It only burns its way back

Put your mind on the future

And it becomes the past

Thinking about love

Hoping it will last

Recreate reality

Slip it within reach

Tangible yet elusive

Holding on with a tight squeeze

Indirectly direct cause and effect

Evaluating life - What is correct?

Seeking stimulation

With numbness nearby

Eyes open wide

The here and now collide

Layers of Woe

Looking thru the window

Past the layers of woe

See you hiding deep inside

pull the blinds open wide

Come closer you know the way out

Feeling unthinking no room for doubt

One foot ahead the other will follow

A heart awaiting no longer hollow

Lift up the sill a little at first

One swift move your freedom will burst

The hand of love will show you the way

In life, in meaning

you are meant to play

Palette of Pleasure

Dipping into my palette of pleasure

Dripping with the colors of love and leisure

Sweet swirling mélange of life

Ridding me of stress and strife

Stroking the brush sensually through

Leaving streaks of erotic hues

Deep and vibrant pulsating forms

Passionate purple peaking storms

Shuddering dimensions waves of light

Affecting my vision affecting my sight

Cobalt blue eyes crimson lips

Soft white skin honey-dripped hips

Slipping and sliding

on dew-kissed grass

Creating the landscape

for love ever last

Love Accrues

Peeking through my silky hair

Looking through eyes that don't mean to stare

Blinking and batting my lashes with flare

At a sensitive man so kind so rare

A heart flushed with crimson hue

Moving closer for a silent view

Whispering sweet as love accrues

Gathering momentum coming true

Straining for the words I long to hear

Your breath tickling my naked ear

I've never experienced something so strong so clear

With you in my heart I have nothing to fear

Shallow Depths

I was talking to nobody

And nobody listened

The depth of the words

Were shallow unheard

When they met the right ears

They relieved all my fears

Falling into your eyes

Letting go of buried sighs

Floating unfocused

Clouded by lust

Wanting to trust

Buzzing Bee

Droning moaning buzzing bee

Flush the rush of a flowing sea

Breeze tickling naked skin

Touch my mind move within

My being whole divided in two

Emotional and physical needs so new

Deciding the straight or crooked path

Feeling encouraged by your laugh

Sleeping waking tired eyes

Questioning the act of parting thighs

Innocence a veil

A heart open yet frail

Receiving invitations

Tempting situations

Feeling lips roving hands

Escalating bodily demands

Dizzy dancing thoughts alit

Swooning surreal intoxicated skit

The players acting like you and me

Unable to be completely free

Guarded with a tear close by

Processing fear with a heavy sigh

Time slipping slowly past

Bringing me closer to love at last

Feet Forward Tears Behind

Floating between here and there

In-void in-limbo kind of scared

Point me towards what I'm meant to see

Show me the future that will set me free

Who, what, when, where, and why

Procession of life, love, and lies

Start to stop finish to begin

Striving to enter, go within

Feet forward tears behind

Clinging longing clearing my mind

Separate the logic memories attached

Questioning combos that never match

Resolve to let go

Feeling God in the flow

No decision to make

Open to whatever is at stake

What is offered in its time

Will be the loving and the divine

Watching from Above

If you were here

What would you say?

Would you be near?

Helping in every way

Nothing compares to you

Watching from above

Below I melt and spew

Longing for the days radiating in your love

Your smile deep in my heart

For the rest of my life

Optical illusion we seem apart

Yet deep and connected, without you I cry

I hear your voice

'Are you happy', you say

Wanting to find the choice

Headed for divorce, grief on display

Where did you go?

Is it a pleasant peaceful place?

Eventually I will know

And then be able to touch your face

Again we will dance

Our spirits infinitely connected

I journey towards the chance

To be with you again selected

No Need to Think

Slippery rope

grabbing hope

Illusive heart

will never part

Connected spirits

dance in sync

Away or near

no need to think

Free-flow exchange

No obstacles of fear

Now is the only time

Love is the only word to hear

Unrestrained

Waiting for

an unknown man

Looking out

across the sands

Of time that goes

Slipping slowly by

The mirage appears

Do not deny

It is you I see

and totally feel

Grabbing my heart

you completely steal

The weather shifts

intense and dramatic

Setting the mood

Feeling romantic

Thunder rumbles

lightening strikes

Urges rising

Thinking alike

Pouring down

wild and wet

Getting all ready

Getting set

Unexpected

newly directed

thoroughly affected

Passion takes hold

unrestrained

There is nothing about this

that can be tamed

Ominous Gaze

There is an ominous gaze

With loving eyes that peer through the haze

When two beings can float and swim

Connected by a beam unleashed from within

Forming the bridge for emotions to glide

So completely open with nothing to hide

Propel and slip deep into your soul

Lighting the flame under the coal

Not a word or syllable

uttered or spoken

Yet the communications

are so strong and unbroken

Somewhere in Space

A permanent smile on my face

My heart floating somewhere in space

My mind's touch to trace

Your image ingrained

Deep in the terrain

Of the recesses of my being

Bright lights flicker inside

When I think of you

I try and decide

Which way this will go

Probably better

Just to let it flow

Let what is meant to be

Naturally unfold for us to see

Stop and Start

Lay your head on my heart

Feel the beats stop and start

My breath flows for you

Exhaling love circling true

A blanket of warmth and security

Floats gently over our souls

Caressing deep a sense of purity

Filling in missing pieces and holes

Wholeness unites us

One being at last

For you I do lust

Erasing my past

Reach out to me

Embrace what I offer

I am the treasure you see

Take the key

Unlock possibilities

Syncopation

Intrinsic timing

Click clock rhyming

Syncopation

Fluid duration

Hours freeze

Minutes in the breeze

Floating past

Hurling future cast

Shadows on the present

Illumination reminiscent

Memory yet to happen

Overlapped and trapping

Now and then

Tell me when

Have we reached the end?

Tongue to Trip

Splendorous rapture

Captures my mind

Tripping on thoughts

I left behind

Thankful and thoughtful

The blessings of life

Fading shadows

Of challenging strife

I need to find just how I feel

Search the recesses for the deal

To convey to my heart and lips

So I speak to you

Without a tongue to trip

The truth is I'm not sure

Lost connection to find the cure

To heal my heart anew

So I can be complete with you

Turmoil Soil

Reflecting on a year of turmoil

The tears fall and dampen the soil

The heavy heart once alone and apart

Rejoices anew with a lover who is true

A journey of emotions have thrown

A new life of challenges and has shown

Me who I can be

What are all the possibilities?

Of growth and expansion

For one individual to explore

With a multitude of decisions

Every one will open a door

It is a matter of choice

Of listening to the voice

That tells me what is right

With God, love, and hope

Always in sight

A Book For Your Healing

Writing is not only Ms. Clemens' art and passion but has also been her therapy. During times of sadness for love that faded away, she turned to her writing as a form of therapy to help process the emotions that filled her head and heart. In this book, she shares with you some of those poems so that you might also process and mend your broken heart.

The poems in this book are a therapeutic diary of love and change. They helped Clarissa to let go, grieve, and feel the hope that propelled her back into love.

This collection of poems is here to help you heal, hold on to all of your hope, and find your way back to love everlasting.

Clarissa O. Clemens